God's Kingdom is at Hand

By Karajah Yashar

BLACKSTONE PUBLISHING

Orlando, FL 2024

Repent
God's Kingdom is at Hand

www.bspbooks.com

ISBN: 978-1-962691-38-3

First Edition: August 2024

Table of Contents

Introduction

Repentance is a fundamental tenet for the disciples of Christ, integral to spiritual growth and a deepening relationship with God. It involves a sincere turning away from sin and a heartfelt commitment to change one's behavior and mindset. The Bible emphasizes the necessity of repentance as a prerequisite for receiving God's grace and forgiveness. In Acts 3:19, Peter exhorts, "Repent ye therefore, and be converted, that your sins may be blotted out, when the times of refreshing shall come from the presence of the Lord." This underscores that repentance is not merely a one-time act but an ongoing process of spiritual renewal and alignment with God's will.

Restoration of Fellowship with God

Repentance restores and enhances our fellowship with God, bridging the gap that sin creates between humanity and the Divine. Sin separates us from God's holiness, leading to spiritual death and estrangement. Through repentance, we acknowledge our sins, seek God's forgiveness, and restore our relationship with Him. 1 John 1:9 assures, "If we confess our sins, he is faithful and just to forgive us our sins, and to cleanse us from all unrighteousness." This cleansing allows believers to walk in the light of God's truth and experience the fullness of His love and grace. Without repentance, we remain burdened by guilt and disconnected from the source of our spiritual life.

Transformation and Renewal

Repentance is crucial for personal transformation and renewal. It initiates a change in heart and mind that leads to a new way of living, reflecting the character and values of Christ. Romans 12:2 instructs, "And be not conformed to this world: but be ye transformed by the renewing of your mind, that ye may prove what is that good, and acceptable, and perfect, will of God." Through repentance, believers are empowered to break free from sinful patterns and embrace a life of righteousness. This transformation is not self-generated but is facilitated by the Holy Spirit, who works within us to produce the fruits of repentance, such as love, joy, peace, and self-control.

Preparation for Eternal Life

Repentance also prepares believers for eternal life, aligning them with the kingdom of God. Jesus' ministry began with a call to repentance, highlighting its importance in entering the kingdom of heaven. Matthew 4:17 records, "From that time Jesus began to preach, and to say, Repent: for the kingdom of heaven is at hand." This call to repentance is a call to readiness, ensuring that our lives are in accordance with God's standards. It is through repentance that we receive the gift of salvation and the promise of eternal life. By turning away from sin and turning towards God, we secure our place in His eternal kingdom and experience the hope and assurance that come with living a life pleasing to Him.

Chapter 1: Defining Repentance

Repentance is a profound and transformative concept central to reconciliation with God and receiving the Kingdom of Heaven. Rooted in the teachings of the Scriptures, repentance involves a sincere turning away from sin and a wholehearted turning towards God. It is more than merely feeling remorseful for one's actions; it encompasses a complete change of heart, mind, and behavior.

Biblical Foundations of Repentance

The concept of repentance is deeply embedded in both the Old and New Testaments. In the Old Testament, the Hebrew word "shuv" is often used to denote repentance, which literally means "to turn back" or "to return." This term is frequently used in the context of Israel turning back to God after straying from His commandments.

For instance, the prophet Isaiah called the people to repentance, urging them to "return unto the LORD, and he will have mercy upon him; and to our God, for he will abundantly pardon" (Isaiah 55:7).

In the New Testament, the Greek word "metanoia" is used, meaning "a change of mind." This concept is epitomized in the teachings of John the Baptist, who preached "the baptism of repentance for the remission of sins" (Mark 1:4). Jesus Himself began His ministry with a call to repentance, stating, "Repent: for the kingdom of heaven is at hand" (Matthew 4:17). This call to repentance is a consistent theme throughout the Gospels and the teachings of the Apostles.

Repentance is a fundamental concept that transcends cultural boundaries, embodying the profound transformation of one's heart and mind. At its core, repentance involves recognizing and feeling remorse for one's wrongdoings, making a commitment to change, and taking active steps to rectify one's behavior.

The Essence of Repentance

Repentance begins with self-awareness and the acknowledgment of one's mistakes or sins. This initial step is crucial, as it requires an honest and often painful self-examination. It is not merely about recognizing that a wrong has been done but involves a deep understanding of why the action was wrong and how it has affected oneself and others. This introspection often leads to a sense of guilt or sorrow, emotions that are integral to genuine repentance.

Emotional and Moral Dimensions

The emotional aspect of repentance is characterized by contrition, which is a heartfelt sorrow for having committed the wrong. This sorrow is not just about fearing punishment or regretting the consequences but stems from a genuine understanding of the harm caused. This sorrow is a necessary precondition for divine forgiveness. "The sacrifices of God are a broken spirit: a broken and a contrite heart, O God, thou wilt not despise" Psalm 51:17.

On a moral level, repentance involves a commitment to change. This is not a mere promise but a profound resolution to turn away from the past behavior and to strive towards a better path. This commitment is often manifested in concrete actions that demonstrate a genuine transformation. It involves three stages: recognizing the sin, feeling remorse, and resolving not to repeat the sin, along with making amends if the sin involved harm to others.

The Role of Confession and Forgiveness

Confession is another critical element of repentance. Confession is a sacrament that involves admitting one's sins to those involved or an ordained counselor. This act of confession is a way to cleanse the soul and restore one's relationship with God. Confession can also be a personal act between the individual and God, often accompanied by prayers of penitence and fasting.

Forgiveness, both seeking it from those wronged and granting it to oneself, is an integral part of repentance. Seeking forgiveness requires humility and the courage to face the consequences of one's actions. It also involves a willingness to make restitution, where possible, to those who have been harmed. Granting oneself forgiveness is equally important, as it allows one to move forward without being paralyzed by guilt and self-reproach.

Repentance as a Continuous Process

Repentance is not a one-time act but a continuous process of self-improvement and moral vigilance. It requires ongoing reflection and a commitment to living in accordance with one's values and principles. The practice of repentance is a way to purify the mind and cultivate a life of virtue and wisdom.

The Broader Implications of Repentance

Beyond its personal dimensions, repentance has broader social and ethical implications. It fosters a culture of accountability and responsibility, encouraging individuals to take ownership of their actions and to work towards healing and reconciliation. In a societal context, collective repentance can play a crucial role in addressing historical injustices and building a more just and compassionate community.

Overview

In essence, repentance is a multifaceted and transformative process that involves recognizing one's wrongdoings, feeling genuine remorse, making a committed effort to change, and seeking forgiveness. It is a journey towards moral integrity and personal growth, deeply rooted in self-awareness and a commitment to living a life of virtue. Whether viewed through a religious, cultural, or philosophical lens, repentance remains a powerful and enduring concept that underscores the importance of humility, accountability, and the continuous pursuit of a better self.

Chapter 2: The Process of Repentance

Repentance is a multifaceted process that involves several key components, each contributing to a profound transformation of the individual. The first component is *recognition of sin* where an individual must recognize and acknowledge their wrongdoing. This initial step requires a deep and honest introspection, often accompanied by a sense of guilt or sorrow for the harm caused. Understanding the nature and impact of one's actions is crucial as it sets the foundation for genuine remorse, which is the second component. This *remorse* is more than just regret; it is a heartfelt sorrow that stems from recognizing the moral or ethical failure of one's actions. It reflects an emotional response that signifies the individual's realization of their fault and the pain it has caused others.

Following this, the third key component is *confession*, where the individual openly admits their fault, to those they have wronged and/or, to a mentor, as well as to God. Confession is a crucial step as it externalizes the internal process of repentance and often paves the way for the fourth component the *turning away from sin*. This involves a determined resolution to turn away from past behaviors and to strive towards better actions in the future. This commitment is often demonstrated through concrete actions aimed at making amends and preventing the recurrence of the wrongdoing. The last component is: *transformation and renewal*. Transformation and renewal in involve a profound shift in an individual's mindset, behavior, and overall outlook on life. As individuals turn away from their previous actions and strive to adopt new, positive behaviors, they undergo a significant personal transformation. This transformation is not just about changing actions but also about cultivating a renewed sense of self-awareness, integrity, and moral clarity. Through continuous self-reflection and effort, repentance leads to the renewal of one's values and principles, ultimately fostering a more authentic and virtuous way of living. This renewal is marked by a deeper understanding of one's impact on others and a strengthened resolve to contribute positively to their community and relationships.

Step 1: Recognition of Sin

Recognition of sin is the initial and critical step in the process of repentance. This acknowledgment involves a profound sense of self-awareness and a clear understanding of how one's actions, thoughts, and attitudes have deviated from God's commandments and will. The Bible emphasizes the importance of this step in passages such as

Psalm 51:3, where David declares, "For I acknowledge my transgressions: and my sin is ever before me." This recognition is not merely a casual admission but a deep realization of one's moral and spiritual failings before a holy God.

The role of the Holy Spirit is indispensable in this process of recognizing sin. Jesus promised the coming of the Holy Spirit to convict the world of sin, righteousness, and judgment (John 16:8). The Holy Spirit illuminates the darkness in our hearts, revealing the areas where we have strayed from God's path. This conviction is a divine intervention that brings to light our need for repentance and reconciliation with God. As the Apostle Paul wrote in Romans 7:7, "I had not known sin, but by the law: for I had not known lust, except the law had said, Thou shalt not covet." The Holy Spirit uses the law to expose sin and make us aware of our guilt.

This awareness of sin leads to an essential turning point where individuals can no longer ignore their moral state. Recognizing one's sin is a humbling experience that strips away self-righteousness and pride. It aligns with the biblical narrative of humankind's need for a Savior, as stated in Romans 3:23, "For all have sinned, and come short of the glory of God." This acknowledgment fosters a sincere desire to seek God's forgiveness and to make amends. The journey of repentance begins with this crucial step, setting the stage for the transformative process that follows, leading to spiritual renewal and a restored relationship with God.

Step 2: Remorse

Remorse, a key aspect of genuine repentance, involves a profound, heartfelt grief over having offended God. This type of remorse goes beyond mere regret or the fear of punishment that often characterizes worldly sorrow. Instead, godly remorse stems from a deep understanding and acknowledgment of one's transgressions against a holy and loving God. This remorse is not just about the consequences of sin, but about the rupture it creates in one's relationship with God. It is a recognition of how sin damages the harmony between the Creator and His creation, and it reflects a sincere desire to restore that relationship.

The Apostle Paul highlights the distinction between godly sorrow and worldly sorrow in his letter to the Corinthians. In 2 Corinthians 7:10, he writes, "For godly sorrow worketh repentance to salvation not to be repented of: but the sorrow of the world worketh death." Paul underscores that while worldly sorrow can lead to despair and spiritual death, godly sorrow leads to repentance and ultimately to salvation. This godly sorrow is transformative, prompting a change of heart and mind that aligns a person more closely with God's will. It is this sincere, contrite heart that God seeks, as stated in Psalm 51:17, "The sacrifices of God are a broken spirit: a broken and a contrite heart, O God, thou wilt not despise."

Furthermore, remorse is a crucial step in the journey of repentance because it fosters genuine humility and dependence on God's grace. When one experiences godly sorrow, there is an acknowledgment of one's inability to achieve righteousness on their own and a deep reliance on God's mercy and forgiveness. This humble posture opens the door to divine transformation, where the Holy Spirit can work within to produce lasting change. It leads to a renewed commitment to live according to God's standards, resulting in a life that bears the fruit of the Spirit. Thus, godly sorrow is not an end in itself but a gateway to a deeper, more authentic relationship with God, characterized by ongoing spiritual growth and renewal.

Step #3: Confession

Confessing one's sins to those harmed and or a mentor as well as to God is a vital aspect of repentance, serving as an acknowledgment of one's wrongdoing and an appeal for divine mercy and forgiveness. This act of confession is a critical step in the process of reconciliation with God, as it demonstrates a sincere recognition of personal sin and a willingness to seek His pardon. Confession is more than a mere admission of guilt; it is a humble acknowledgment of having done wrong and violating God's commandments and an earnest plea for His grace. Through confession, believers openly admit their shortcomings, paving the way for spiritual healing and restoration.

The Bible underscores the importance of confession in the journey of repentance. In 1 John 1:9, believers are given a profound assurance: "If we confess our sins, he is faithful and just to forgive us our sins, and to cleanse us from all unrighteousness." This promise highlights God's unwavering faithfulness and justice in forgiving those who come to Him with a contrite heart. By confessing their sins, individuals experience the cleansing power of God's forgiveness, which removes the stain of sin and restores them to a state of righteousness. This divine promise offers hope and encouragement, assuring believers that no sin is too great to be forgiven when genuinely confessed.

When believers confess their sins, they acknowledge their dependence on God's grace and mercy, recognizing that they cannot attain righteousness on their own.

This humble admission strengthens their connection with other people and God, as it is rooted in trust and a desire for spiritual renewal. Confession also cultivates a spirit of humility and accountability, reminding believers of their need for ongoing repentance and transformation. As they regularly confess their sins, they grow in their understanding of God's love and grace, leading to a more profound and authentic faith journey.

James 5:16 states: "Confess *your* faults one to another, and pray one for another, that ye may be healed. The effectual fervent prayer of a righteous man availeth much." Confession earns people's respect and trust by demonstrating honesty, accountability, and a genuine commitment to change. It shows that the individual is willing to own up to their mistakes and take the necessary steps to make amends, fostering a sense of integrity and reliability in their character.

Step #4: Turning Away from Sin

Turning away from sin is a fundamental component of repentance, marking a decisive break from behaviors, thoughts, and attitudes that are contrary to God's commandments. This aspect of repentance goes beyond mere acknowledgment of sin and regret; it involves a conscious, intentional decision to renounce sinful ways. In making this choice, individuals demonstrate a genuine desire to align their lives with God's standards of holiness and righteousness. This turning away from sin signifies a critical shift in one's spiritual journey, redirecting focus from self-centered desires to a God-centered life.

This conscious decision to turn away from sin is not solely about stopping harmful actions but also about transforming one's mindset and heart. It requires a commitment to reject thoughts and attitudes that lead to sin, such as pride, lust, greed, and envy. Instead, believers are called to embrace the virtues and values that reflect God's character. The Apostle Paul emphasizes this transformation in Romans 12:2, urging believers, "And be not conformed to this world: but be ye transformed by the renewing of your mind, that ye may prove what is that good, and acceptable, and perfect, will of God." Turning away from sin, therefore, involves a holistic change that encompasses both external actions and internal dispositions.

Coupled with this renunciation of sin is a commitment to pursue righteousness and live according to God's will. This pursuit involves actively seeking to embody the teachings of Jesus and the principles of God's laws and commandments in daily life. It means striving to cultivate a character that reflects the fruits of the Spirit, such as love, joy, peace, patience, kindness, goodness, faithfulness, gentleness, and self-control (Galatians 5:22-23). Pursuing righteousness is an ongoing process, requiring continual growth, prayer, and reliance on the Holy Spirit for strength and guidance. By turning away from sin and dedicating oneself to a righteous path, believers not only honor God but also experience the fullness of life that comes from living in harmony with His will.

Step #5: Transformation and Renewal

True repentance results in a profound transformation of the heart and mind, marking the beginning of a renewed relationship with God. This change is not superficial but deeply rooted in a sincere commitment to live according to God's will. When an individual genuinely repents, they undergo a spiritual renewal that affects every aspect of their being. This transformation involves a shift in priorities, values, and behaviors, aligning them more closely with God's commandments and desires. It is a process of becoming more like Christ, as believers strive to embody His love, grace, and holiness in their daily lives.

The Apostle Paul vividly describes this transformation in his letter to the Ephesians, urging believers to "put off concerning the former conversation the old man, which is corrupt according to the deceitful lusts; and be renewed in the spirit of your mind; and that ye put on the new man, which after God is created in righteousness and true holiness" (Ephesians 4:22-24). This passage emphasizes the importance of abandoning the old self, characterized by sinful desires and behaviors, and embracing a new identity in Christ. This new self is created in the likeness of God, reflecting His righteousness and holiness. It signifies a complete overhaul of one's inner life, leading to outward changes that are evident to others.

Transformation and renewal through repentance lead to a life that increasingly mirrors God's character. As believers grow in their faith, they become more attuned to the leading of the Holy Spirit, who empowers them to live out their new identity in Christ. This journey of transformation is ongoing, requiring continual surrender to God's will and a commitment to spiritual growth. As they put off the old self and put on the new, believers experience the joy and freedom that come from living in harmony with God's purposes. Their lives become a testimony to the transformative power of God's grace, inspiring others to seek the same renewal and relationship with Him.

Chapter 3: The Fruits of Repentance

Repentance is not an isolated event but an ongoing process in the life of a believer. Its fruits are evident in a transformed character and conduct. Genuine repentance leads to a deeper intimacy with God, greater spiritual maturity, and an increased capacity to love and serve others. This continuous process of turning away from sin and seeking God's forgiveness brings about a profound change in a person's life, fostering qualities such as humility, compassion, and a strong sense of moral responsibility. The transformation is not just internal but also external, as it manifests in actions that reflect a renewed commitment to living in accordance with divine principles.

One of the most significant fruits of repentance is the deepened intimacy with God. As believers turn away from sin and draw closer to God, they experience a profound sense of peace and connection with the divine. This closeness to God enhances their spiritual maturity, enabling them to understand and apply spiritual truths more effectively in their lives. The increased capacity to love and serve others is another key outcome of genuine repentance. As believers grow in their relationship with God, they become more attuned to the needs of those around them, often leading to acts of kindness, generosity, and service that reflect God's love.

Repentance and a deeper intimacy with God lead to true joy, a joy that surpasses the fleeting pleasures of worldly pursuits. Many people seek continual short-term gratification through material possessions, food, sex, status, or other temporary thrills. However, these momentary pleasures pale in comparison to the profound and lasting joy that comes from a relationship with God. True joy, rooted in the assurance of God's love and forgiveness, provides a sense of fulfillment and contentment that is far superior to any transient excitement. This joy is a testament to the transformative power of repentance, as it brings believers into a closer relationship with God and a deeper understanding of their purpose and identity in Him.

The Thrills of Sin

Many people entertain their demons, mistakenly believing they are sources of fun and excitement. Substance abuse, sexual perversions, and other carnal indulgences become perceived as essential components of an exhilarating life. These behaviors, often glamorized by society and media, create a false sense of fulfillment and pleasure. The immediate gratification they provide blinds individuals to the long-term consequences and spiritual emptiness that accompany such lifestyles. In this pursuit of fleeting thrills, the concept of repentance seems unappealing and unnecessary, as the superficial joy derived from sinful behaviors appears more attractive than the perceived austerity of a righteous life.

The chaos and drama resulting from these sins are often misconstrued as excitement, leading individuals to equate turmoil with vitality. The rollercoaster of emotions, conflicts, and adrenaline rushes stemming from substance abuse or illicit relationships can create a semblance of vibrancy in one's life. This constant state of turmoil becomes addictive, making the idea of a stable, drama-free existence seem dull by comparison. For many, the allure of this chaotic lifestyle overshadows the destructive impact it has on their mental, emotional, and physical well-being. They become trapped in a cycle of seeking out these destructive pleasures, reinforcing their resistance to repentance and change.

The notion that being good and drama-free is boring stems from a misunderstanding of what true joy and peace entail. Living in alignment with moral and spiritual principles does not equate to a monotonous or unfulfilling life. Instead, it offers a deep, abiding sense of peace and satisfaction that far surpasses the temporary highs of sinful behaviors. If individuals could experience the profound joy and serenity that come from a relationship with the Lord, they would realize how hollow their previous pursuits were. The joy of the Lord brings clarity, purpose, and contentment that chaotic lifestyles can never match, illuminating the stark contrast between temporary thrills and lasting happiness.

If people truly felt the joy and peace of the Lord, the decision to flee from their destructive behaviors would be crystal clear. The transformative power of divine joy and peace reveals the emptiness of carnal pleasures and the chaos they bring. Experiencing the fullness of life that comes from living in harmony with God's will exposes the lie that sinful behaviors are fun or necessary for a fulfilling life. This divine joy fosters a genuine desire for repentance, as individuals recognize the superior value of a life rooted in spiritual wholeness over one mired in transient, destructive thrills. Repentance then becomes not just a moral obligation but a liberating step towards true happiness and fulfillment.

Heaven vs Hell

In the long term, the Kingdom of Heaven is far superior to the pits of hell, highlighting the serious consequences of non-repentance. Hell, a place of eternal separation from God and suffering, is the ultimate outcome for those who choose not to repent. The afterlife offers two starkly contrasting destinations: Heaven as the reward for the righteous and hell as the consequence for the unrepentant. Stories of near-death experiences, where individuals report visions of heaven and hell, often reinforce the reality of these eternal destinies. These accounts serve as powerful reminders of the importance of repentance and the eternal significance of one's choices in this life.

The Choice is Clear

Ultimately, the fruits of repentance extend beyond personal transformation to impact the broader community and the world. A repentant heart, attuned to God's will and committed to living out His principles, becomes a powerful witness to the transformative power of God's grace. This witness can inspire others to seek repentance and experience their own journey of renewal and transformation. In this way, the ongoing process of repentance not only brings about individual spiritual growth but also contributes to the collective well-being and moral integrity of society. The fruits of repentance, therefore, are manifold, encompassing personal joy, deeper intimacy with God, and a positive influence on the world.

Repentance is a foundational aspect of righteous living, encapsulating the essence of spiritual renewal and transformation. The fruits of repentance are evident in a changed life that reflects God's love and righteousness. Through repentance, believers experience the joy of forgiveness and the assurance of eternal life, reaffirming the hope and promise of the Gospel.

Chapter 4: Substance Abuse

"Be sober, be vigilant; because your adversary the devil, as a roaring lion, walketh about, seeking whom he may devour" 1 Peter 5:8

Substance abuse, including addiction to drugs, cigarettes, marijuana, and alcohol, is a significant area where repentance is necessary. These behaviors not only harm an individual's physical and mental health but also strain relationships and hinder one's spiritual growth. In the context of living holy, addiction represents a formidable barrier to living a life aligned with the teachings and values of Christ. It becomes an idol, taking precedence over one's relationship with God, and requires a profound process of repentance to overcome.

Substance abuse damages the body, which is the temple of the Holy Spirit. The Apostle

Paul writes in 1 Corinthians 6:19-20, "Do you not know that your bodies are temples of the Holy Spirit, who is in you, whom you have received from God? You are not your own; you were bought at a price. Therefore honor God with your bodies." Addiction not only defiles the physical body but also hampers mental well-being, leading to a cycle of dependency that is difficult to break. This physical and mental deterioration is compounded by the spiritual distance that substance abuse creates between the individual and God.

Moreover, substance abuse strains relationships with family, friends, and the broader community. The destructive behaviors associated with addiction, such as lying, stealing, and neglecting responsibilities, erode trust and create conflict. These strained relationships further alienate individuals from the communal aspect of faith, which emphasizes love, support, and accountability. The Bible teaches the importance of loving one another and bearing each other's burdens (Galatians 6:2), principles that are undermined by the isolating nature of addiction.

Repenting from substance abuse involves a multifaceted approach. The first step is acknowledging the destructive nature of the addiction and the impact it has on one's life and relationships. This requires humility and a willingness to confront the problem honestly. Seeking help is essential, whether through counseling, support groups, or medical intervention. These practical steps are vital, but they must be coupled with a spiritual turning back to God. Prayer, reading Scripture, and participating in a faith community provide the spiritual support necessary for overcoming addiction.

Turning to God for strength and healing is central to the repentance process. Jesus said in Matthew 11:28-30, "Come to me, all you who are weary and burdened, and I will give you rest. Take my yoke upon you and learn from me, for I am gentle and humble in heart, and you will find rest for your souls. For my yoke is easy and my burden is light." This invitation to find rest and healing in Christ is a promise of the support and strength needed to overcome addiction. Embracing a sober life aligned with the values of discipleship opens the door to true freedom and a deeper connection with Christ.

Repentance from substance abuse is not just about quitting harmful behaviors but about embracing a new way of life that honors God. It involves a transformation that reorients priorities, placing God at the center. This transformation leads to spiritual growth, as individuals learn to rely on God's strength rather than their own. It fosters a sense of peace and fulfillment that substance abuse can never provide. As individuals grow closer to Christ, they experience the fruits of the Spirit, such as love, joy, peace, and self-control (Galatians 5:22-23), which replace the chaos and emptiness of addiction.

Marijuana addiction is often downplayed due to its widespread acceptance and legalization in many areas, but it presents significant challenges and dangers. One of the primary issues with marijuana addiction is the financial strain it can place on individuals. Regular users may find themselves spending money on the drug that is needed for essential expenses like bills, groceries, and other household needs. This can lead to financial instability and stress, affecting both the individual and their loved ones. Additionally, marijuana use often causes drowsiness and laziness, impairing productivity and motivation. This can result in poor performance at work or school, and the neglect of important responsibilities.

Furthermore, marijuana use can lead to delusional 'high thoughts' and altered perceptions, which may open the door to negative spiritual influences. These altered states of consciousness can make individuals more susceptible to harmful ideologies and behaviors that they would typically avoid. The physical act of smoking marijuana also poses health risks, particularly to the lungs. The smoke can damage the delicate pink tissue of the lungs, increasing the risk of respiratory issues and chronic conditions over time. Despite its reputation as a relatively harmless substance, marijuana addiction can have far-reaching consequences that affect every aspect of a person's life, emphasizing the need for awareness and caution.

Rebirth in Christ and a strong support system has often been the most effective way for individuals to give up highly addictive substances such as cigarettes, heroin, and crack. This transformative experience offers a profound sense of purpose and a renewed identity, empowering individuals to break free from the chains of addiction. When people accept Christ into their lives, they often experience a radical shift in their values and priorities, making it easier to resist the temptations of addictive substances. The strength and support derived from a personal relationship with Jesus provide a powerful foundation for overcoming addiction. Through prayer, scripture, and fellowship with other believers, individuals find the spiritual resources and community support necessary to embark on and sustain their journey toward recovery.

Moreover, rebirth in Christ brings about a deep sense of hope and healing that many find crucial in their fight against addiction. Christ emphasizes forgiveness and redemption, allowing individuals to leave behind their past mistakes and embrace a new life. This sense of spiritual renewal often translates into practical steps toward sobriety, as individuals feel motivated to honor their bodies as temples of the Holy Spirit and live in a way that reflects their new faith. Testimonies abound of former addicts who, through their newfound faith in Christ, have not only conquered their addictions but also transformed their lives, finding meaning, purpose, and joy that far surpass the fleeting highs of substance use. The holistic transformation that comes with rebirth in Christ addresses the root causes of addiction and provides a comprehensive pathway to lasting recovery.

Chapter 5: Sexual Perversions

"Flee fornication. Every sin that a man doeth is without the body; but he that committeth fornication sinneth against his own body."
1 Corinthians 6:18

The Bible's stance on sexual perversions such as premarital sex, homosexuality, and sodomy is unequivocal. These behaviors are consistently portrayed as violations of God's design for human sexuality and are met with strong condemnation. The call to sexual purity is a recurring theme throughout Scripture, urging believers to honor God with their bodies and to uphold the sanctity of marriage. While the Bible's teachings may seem stringent, they are rooted in the belief that adhering to God's commandments leads to a more fulfilling and spiritually aligned life. As such, believers are encouraged to seek forgiveness, embrace repentance, and strive to live according to the divine standards set forth in Scripture.

Fornication

Fornication, defined as engaging in sexual relations outside the bounds of marriage, is a significant in our modern world. The Bible consistently addresses and condemns this behavior, emphasizing the spiritual and physical ramifications of such actions. One of the clearest and most direct admonitions against fornication is found in 1 Corinthians 7:1-2: "Now concerning the things whereof ye wrote unto me: It is good for a man not to touch a woman. Nevertheless, to avoid fornication, let every man have his own wife, and let every woman have her own husband."

The Spiritual Consequences of Fornication

From a Biblical perspective, fornication is more than just a physical act; it is a sin that has profound spiritual consequences. The call to "flee fornication" is an urgent directive to avoid actions that can corrupt one's spiritual state. The Apostle Paul highlights the uniqueness of sexual sin by noting that it is a sin against one's own body. This is significant because the body is the temple of the Holy Spirit. When a believer engages in fornication, they defile this sacred temple, thereby dishonoring God who resides within them. This concept is reinforced in Romans 12:1, where believers are urged to present their bodies as a "living sacrifice, holy, acceptable unto God, which is your reasonable service."

The spiritual harm caused by fornication extends to one's relationship with God. Sin creates a barrier between the individual and the divine, disrupting the fellowship and communion that is essential to a vibrant spiritual life. By engaging in sexual immorality, believers distance themselves from God's presence and grieve the Holy Spirit, as mentioned in Ephesians 4:30 : "And grieve not the holy Spirit of God, whereby ye are sealed unto the day of redemption." Therefore, fornication is not merely a breach of moral conduct but a severe offense that impacts one's spiritual standing and relationship with God.

The Physical and Emotional Impact

In addition to the spiritual consequences, fornication also has tangible physical and emotional repercussions. Paul's assertion that "he that committeth fornication sinneth against his own body" underscores the inherent risks associated with sexual immorality. These risks include sexually transmitted infections (STIs), unintended pregnancies, and the emotional turmoil that often accompanies casual sexual relationships. The Bible's prohibition against fornication is thus seen not only as a moral directive but also as a means of protecting individuals from the harmful effects of sexual promiscuity.

Emotionally, fornication can lead to feelings of guilt, shame, and regret. These negative emotions can have long-lasting effects on an individual's mental health and well-being. The temporary pleasure derived from sexual activity outside of marriage often gives way to deeper emotional distress, as individuals grapple with the consequences of their actions. This emotional toll can affect one's self-esteem, relationships, and overall quality of life. The Bible's emphasis on sexual purity aims to safeguard individuals from these detrimental outcomes and promote a sense of wholeness and integrity.

The Call to Purity and Holiness
The Biblical mandate to flee fornication is part of a broader call to purity and holiness.

Believers are exhorted to live lives that reflect God's holiness and to abstain from behaviors that are inconsistent with His nature. 1 Peter 1:15-16 declares, "But as he which hath called you is holy, so be ye holy in all manner of conversation; Because it is written, Be ye holy; for I am holy." This call to holiness extends to all areas of life, including one's sexual conduct. By abstaining from fornication, believers honor God with their bodies and demonstrate their commitment to living according to His standards.

The pursuit of purity is not only a personal endeavor but also a testament to the transformative power of the Gospel. When believers choose to flee fornication and embrace God's design for sexuality, they bear witness to the world of the radical change that Christ brings into a person's life. This commitment to purity serves as a powerful testimony of faith and can inspire others to seek the same transformation in their own lives.

Homosexuality

Homosexuality is another area where the Bible provides explicit guidance, condemning it as contrary to God's natural order. In the Old Testament, Leviticus 18:22 clearly states, "Thou shalt not lie with mankind, as with womankind: it is abomination." This prohibition reflects the truth that homosexual acts disrupt the divinely ordained structure of human sexuality, which is intended to be expressed within heterosexual marriage.

The New Testament reinforces this stance. In Romans 1:26-27, Paul describes homosexual behavior as a consequence of turning away from God: "For this cause God gave them up unto vile affections: for even their women did change the natural use into that which is against nature: And likewise also the men, leaving the natural use of the woman, burned in their lust one toward another; men with men working that which is unseemly, and receiving in themselves that recompence of their error which was meet." This passage associates homosexual acts with a rejection of God's design and warns of the inherent consequences of such behavior.

Sodomy

Sodomy, often used in a broader sense to refer to various forms of sexual perversion, particularly anal intercourse, is similarly condemned in the Bible. The term itself is derived from the biblical account of Sodom and Gomorrah, cities destroyed by God due to their inhabitants' grievous sins, including sexual immorality. In Genesis 19:4-5, the men of Sodom's intent to engage in homosexual acts with Lot's visitors is described: "But before they lay down, the men of the city, even the men of Sodom, compassed the house round, both old and young, all the people from every quarter: And they called unto Lot, and said unto him, Where are the men which came in to thee this night? bring them out unto us, that we may know them." This incident underscores the severity with which God views such acts, leading to the cities' ultimate destruction as a divine judgment.

In the New Testament, 1 Corinthians 6:9-10 further reinforces the condemnation of sodomy and other sexual sins: "Know ye not that the unrighteous shall not inherit the kingdom of God? Be not deceived: neither fornicators, nor idolaters, nor adulterers, nor effeminate, nor abusers of themselves with mankind, Nor thieves, nor covetous, nor drunkards, nor revilers, nor extortioners, shall inherit the kingdom of God." This passage explicitly lists those who engage in various forms of sexual immorality, including sodomy, as being excluded from the kingdom of God, emphasizing the necessity of repentance and a return to righteousness.

Adultery

Adultery, defined as having sexual relations with someone who is not one's spouse, is a grave sin in the Biblical context. The seventh commandment in Exodus 20:14 unequivocally states, "Thou shalt not commit adultery." This commandment underscores the sanctity of marriage and the seriousness with which God views the marital covenant. Adultery violates the exclusive bond between husband and wife, undermining the trust and fidelity that are foundational to a healthy marriage. This act of betrayal not only causes emotional pain and relational strife but also carries significant spiritual consequences.

The Bible repeatedly emphasizes the destructive nature of adultery and its far-reaching implications. In Proverbs 6:32, it is written, "But whoso committeth adultery with a woman lacketh understanding: he that doeth it destroyeth his own soul." This verse highlights the self-destructive nature of adultery, suggesting that those who engage in it are not only harming their spouses but also inflicting damage upon their own souls. The consequences of adultery extend beyond the immediate physical act, leading to a deterioration of one's moral and spiritual integrity. The violation of this sacred trust is seen as an affront to God, who instituted marriage as a holy union between a man and a woman.

In the New Testament, Jesus expands on the commandment against adultery, emphasizing that it is not just the physical act that matters but also the intentions of the heart. In Matthew 5:27-28, Jesus teaches, "Ye have heard that it was said by them of old time, Thou shalt not commit adultery: But I say unto you, That whosoever looketh on a woman to lust after her hath committed adultery with her already in his heart." This teaching highlights the importance of purity of thought and intention, recognizing that sin begins in the heart and mind. By addressing the root causes of adultery—lust and covetousness—Jesus calls His followers to a higher standard of holiness and integrity.

Adultery is not only a personal sin but also a social one, affecting families and communities. The ripple effects of adultery can lead to broken homes, strained relationships, and a breakdown of societal values. The Bible advocates for strong, faithful marriages as the cornerstone of a stable and moral society. Hebrews 13:4 reinforces this, stating, "Marriage is honourable in all, and the bed undefiled: but whoremongers and adulterers God will judge." This verse reiterates the honor and sanctity of marriage, warning of the divine judgment awaiting those who defile it through adultery. The call to faithfulness in marriage is a call to uphold God's design for human relationships, promoting love, trust, and mutual respect.

Incest

Incest, defined as sexual relations with close family members, is explicitly prohibited in the Bible and is considered a serious sin. Leviticus 18:6-18 provides a detailed list of prohibitions against uncovering the nakedness of close relatives, reflecting God's clear directives to maintain the purity and sanctity of familial relationships. These verses state, "None of you shall approach to any that is near of kin to him, to uncover their nakedness: I am the LORD." The specific prohibitions include relationships with one's mother, father, stepmother, sister, half-sister, granddaughter, aunt, step daughter, and daughter-in-law, among others. These laws underscore the importance of respecting family boundaries and preserving the integrity of the family unit.

The prohibition of incest in the Bible serves several important purposes. First, it protects the family structure, which is foundational to societal stability and moral order. Sexual relations within the family can lead to significant emotional and psychological harm, disrupting the trust and bonds that hold families together. By clearly delineating acceptable and unacceptable sexual relationships, the Bible seeks to safeguard the emotional well-being of individuals and maintain the family as a safe and nurturing environment. Incestuous relationships are seen as a violation of the natural order established by God, leading to dysfunction and moral decay. The prohibition of incest is not only a matter of personal and familial ethics but also a vital aspect of maintaining communal holiness and obedience to God.

Bestiality

Bestiality, the act of engaging in sexual relations with animals, is explicitly condemned in the Bible. Leviticus 18:23 (KJV) states, "Neither shalt thou lie with any beast to defile thyself therewith." This prohibition underscores the gravity of such actions, categorizing them as a profound defilement. The biblical mandate against bestiality serves to uphold the natural order and dignity of both humans and animals, reflecting God's design for sexual relations to be confined within the human species and within the sanctity of marriage. Engaging in bestiality is viewed as a perversion of God's creation, leading to moral and spiritual corruption. This commandment is part of a broader framework of laws intended to maintain the holiness and purity of God's people, distinguishing them from the surrounding pagan cultures that may have practiced such abominations. The Bible's clear stance against bestiality is a call to respect the boundaries established by God, promoting a life of integrity and holiness.

Pornography

Pornography, the consumption or production of explicit sexual material, is strongly condemned in the Bible as it directly contradicts the call to purity and holiness in thought and action. In Matthew 5:28, Jesus teaches, "But I say unto you, That whosoever looketh on a woman to lust after her hath committed adultery with her already in his heart." This verse underscores the importance of maintaining purity not just in physical actions but also in one's thoughts and intentions. Pornography fuels lust, which Jesus equates to committing adultery in one's heart, thus highlighting the serious moral and spiritual implications of engaging with such material. It corrupts the mind, distorts God's design for sexuality, and undermines the sanctity of marriage by promoting unrealistic and sinful views of sexual relationships.

The detrimental effects of pornography extend beyond individual spiritual harm, affecting relationships and society as a whole. It often leads to addiction, desensitization, and the objectification of individuals, reducing them to mere objects of sexual gratification rather than respecting their inherent dignity as created in God's image. This can erode trust and intimacy within marriages and relationships, leading to emotional and relational strife. Furthermore, the pornography industry is frequently associated with exploitation and abuse, contributing to broader societal issues such as human trafficking and the degradation of moral standards. By condemning pornography, the Bible calls believers to pursue a life of purity, uphold the sanctity of human sexuality, and foster healthy, respectful relationships that honor God.

Rape

Rape, the act of forcing someone to engage in sexual acts against their will, is unequivocally condemned in the Bible as a grievous sin and a violation of human dignity. Deuteronomy 22:25-27 addresses the gravity of this crime, prescribing severe consequences for the perpetrator: "But if a man find a betrothed damsel in the field, and the man force her, and lie with her: then the man only that lay with her shall die: But unto the damsel thou shalt do nothing; there is in the damsel no sin worthy of death: for as when a man riseth against his neighbour, and slayeth him, even so is this matter: For he found her in the field, and the betrothed damsel cried, and there was none to save her." This passage underscores the seriousness with which rape is regarded, equating it to murder in its violence and injustice. The Bible's laws concerning rape emphasize the protection and vindication of the victim while ensuring that the offender faces just punishment. This reflects the broader Biblical principle of justice and the sanctity of each person's body and autonomy, affirming that any act of sexual violence is a profound offense against both the victim and God.

Prostitution

Prostitution, the act of engaging in sexual acts in exchange for money or goods, is consistently condemned in the Bible as morally degrading and spiritually destructive. Proverbs 23:27 warns, "For a whore is a deep ditch; and a strange woman is a narrow pit." This vivid imagery highlights the dangers and entrapments associated with prostitution, depicting it as a perilous and degrading path that leads to ruin. The act of selling one's body for monetary gain not only diminishes the inherent dignity of the individual but also corrupts the sanctity of human sexuality, which God intended to be expressed within the bounds of a committed marriage relationship. Moreover, prostitution often perpetuates cycles of exploitation and abuse, harming both the individuals involved and the broader community. By denouncing prostitution, the Bible calls for a society that respects and upholds the dignity and purity of each person, promoting relationships that reflect God's love and holiness.

Pedophilia

Pedophilia, the act of engaging in sexual acts with minors, is unequivocally condemned in the Bible as a grave sin and a severe violation of innocence and trust. Mark 9:42 sternly warns, "And whosoever shall offend one of these little ones that believe in me, it is better for him that a millstone were hanged about his neck, and he were cast into the sea." This powerful imagery underscores the profound severity of harming children, highlighting the weight of divine judgment against such offenses. Pedophilia is a reprehensible act that exploits the vulnerability of minors, causing lasting physical, emotional, and psychological damage. It corrupts the inherent purity and trust of children, whom Jesus holds in high regard, and stands in stark opposition to the Biblical mandate to protect and nurture the innocent. By condemning pedophilia, the Bible calls for the safeguarding of children and the upholding of their dignity and innocence, reflecting God's deep concern for their well-being and flourishing.

Overcoming Lust

Overcoming lust involves a multifaceted approach that integrates spiritual transformation, counseling, and an understanding of emotional needs. Spiritual transformation is central to addressing lust, as it involves renewing one's heart and mind to align with God's will. In Romans 12:2 , Paul exhorts believers to "be not conformed to this world: but be ye transformed by the renewing of your mind, that ye may prove what is that good, and acceptable, and perfect, will of God." This transformation begins with a sincere commitment to seek God's guidance through prayer, meditation on Scripture, and the pursuit of holiness. By cultivating a deep relationship with God and allowing His Spirit to work within, individuals can develop a greater capacity to resist temptations and cultivate purity in their thoughts and actions.

Counseling plays a crucial role in overcoming lust, as it provides a structured environment for addressing underlying issues and developing healthier coping strategies. Professional counseling can help individuals identify and confront the root causes of their lustful tendencies, which may include past trauma, unresolved emotional conflicts, or unhealthy patterns of behavior. Through counseling, individuals can gain insights into their behavior, learn practical tools for managing temptation, and receive support in developing healthier relationships and habits. Engaging with a counselor or therapist who understands the spiritual and psychological dimensions of lust can facilitate a more holistic and effective healing process.

Understanding emotional needs is another key aspect of overcoming lust. Often, lustful behavior is a response to unmet emotional needs or a desire for validation and connection. By exploring and addressing these deeper emotional needs, individuals can find healthier ways to fulfill their desires for intimacy and belonging. Building supportive relationships, engaging in meaningful community activities, and developing a strong sense of self-worth rooted in God's love can help individuals find fulfillment and reduce reliance on lustful behaviors. Recognizing and addressing these emotional needs allows individuals to build a more balanced and emotionally healthy life, aligning their desires with God's plan and fostering lasting personal growth.

Chapter 6: Lying

"Lying lips are abomination to the LORD: but they that deal truly are his delight."
Proverbs 12:22

Dishonesty, encompassing lying, deceit, and a lack of integrity in words and actions, is condemned throughout the Bible as fundamentally opposed to God's nature and the principles of righteous living. Exodus 20:16 provides a clear directive: "Thou shalt not bear false witness against thy neighbour." This commandment, part of the Ten Commandments, establishes the foundational principle that honesty and truthfulness are essential to living a life that honors God and respects others. Dishonesty undermines the trust that is crucial for healthy relationships and societal functioning, and its consequences extend far beyond mere misstatements, impacting the very fabric of communal and personal integrity.

The Spiritual and Moral Implications of Dishonesty

Dishonesty is more than a social or ethical issue; it carries profound spiritual implications. The Proverbs 12:22 verse stating "Lying lips are abomination to the LORD: but they that deal truly are his delight" reflects the gravity with which God views dishonesty, describing it as an abomination—a term denoting something detestable and profoundly offensive to God. The Bible presents honesty as a reflection of God's own character, as seen in Titus 1:2, which states, "In hope of eternal life, which God, that cannot lie, promised before the world began." God's nature is inherently truthful, and His people are called to mirror this divine characteristic. Dishonesty disrupts the moral order established by God, leading individuals away from truth and righteousness and creating barriers to genuine relationship and trust.

The Impact of Dishonesty on Relationships and Society

Dishonesty has far-reaching effects on personal relationships and societal integrity. In interpersonal contexts, deceit and lying erode trust, which is essential for maintaining healthy, functional relationships. Proverbs 26:28 warns, "A lying tongue hateth those that are afflicted by it; and a flattering mouth worketh ruin." When individuals engage in dishonesty, they harm others by betraying their trust and undermining the foundation of their interactions. This damage can result in broken relationships, emotional distress, and long-term repercussions that affect the stability and harmony of communities. On a broader scale, widespread dishonesty within a society can lead to systemic issues such as corruption, injustice, and a breakdown of social cohesion, as integrity and transparency are critical for just and functional societal systems.

The Path to Integrity and Truthfulness

Addressing dishonesty involves a commitment to personal integrity and truthfulness. The Bible encourages believers to pursue a life of honesty by reflecting on their own behavior and seeking transformation through God's grace. Ephesians 4:25 exhorts, "Wherefore putting away lying, speak every man truth with his neighbour: for we are members one of another." This directive calls for a conscious effort to reject dishonesty and embrace truthfulness in all interactions. Personal integrity is developed through a consistent practice of honesty, accountability, and repentance. By aligning their words and actions with the truth, individuals can restore trust, foster genuine relationships, and contribute to a more just and harmonious society.

In summary, dishonesty—manifested in lying, deceit, and a lack of integrity—stands in direct opposition to Biblical teachings and divine character. Exodus 20:16 and related scriptures underscore the importance of truthfulness and the severe implications of dishonesty. Addressing dishonesty requires a commitment to spiritual and moral transformation, a dedication to maintaining trust in relationships, and an understanding of the broader impact of integrity on society. By striving to live in accordance with God's standards of truth and honesty, individuals can contribute to a more righteous and equitable world, reflecting the divine nature of God in their daily lives.

Chapter 7: Gluttony and Over Eating

"And put a knife to thy throat, if thou be a man given to appetite." Proverbs 23:2

Gluttony, characterized by overindulgence in food, drink, or other pleasures, is condemned in the Bible as a form of excess that undermines spiritual and physical well-being. Proverbs 23:20-21 warns, "Be not among winebibbers; among riotous eaters of flesh: For the drunkard and the glutton shall come to poverty: and drowsiness shall clothe a man with rags." This passage highlights the dangers of overindulgence, associating it with poverty and ruin. Gluttony is not merely a personal failing but a moral and spiritual issue that reflects a lack of self-control and disregard for the body as a temple of the Holy Spirit. The Bible advocates for moderation and self-discipline, urging believers to respect their bodies and avoid the pitfalls of excessive pleasure.

The Impact of Gluttony on Modern Health and Well-being

In contemporary society, gluttony manifests in various forms, including overeating, addiction to sugary and greasy foods, and unhealthy lifestyles. The rise of obesity and related health issues, such as diabetes and cardiovascular diseases, is a modern testament to the consequences of gluttony. Excessive consumption of high-calorie, processed foods laden with sugar, salt, and unhealthy fats has become a prevalent issue, contributing to widespread health problems. This addiction to unhealthy foods mirrors the Biblical warnings against overindulgence and highlights the need for a balanced approach to eating and living. The Bible's call for moderation and respect for the body as a holy temple remains relevant, urging individuals to adopt healthier lifestyles and avoid the destructive patterns associated with gluttony.

The Role of Pagan Holidays in Encouraging Gluttony

Pagan holidays and celebrations often exacerbate the tendency towards gluttony, as these events typically involve excessive food and drink. Festivities such as Halloween, Christmas, and various national holidays are marked by elaborate feasts and indulgent treats, which can lead to overconsumption and a lack of self-control.

The Bible instructs believers to avoid celebrating paganism and adhering to the traditions of man that deviate from God's commandments. In Jeremiah 10:2, the Lord commands, "Thus saith the LORD, Learn not the way of the heathen, and be not dismayed at the signs of heaven; for the heathen are dismayed at them." This directive emphasizes the importance of not adopting the practices and customs of pagan cultures, which often conflict with divine principles.

Additionally, in Colossians 2:8, Paul warns, "Beware lest any man spoil you through philosophy and vain deceit, after the tradition of men, after the rudiments of the world, and not after Christ." This verse highlights the danger of following human traditions that are contrary to the teachings of Christ, urging believers to remain steadfast in their faith and adhere to Biblical principles rather than secular or pagan practices. The Bible consistently calls for a separation from worldly influences that contradict God's holiness, encouraging a focus on worship and practices that honor Him alone.

Pagan festivities present opportunities for people to engage in gluttonous behavior, reflecting a cultural tendency to live to eat rather than eat to live. The overindulgence observed during these times is a reminder of the broader societal issues related to gluttony and the need for mindful and responsible eating habits. Biblical Holidays such as Passover and Pentecost do not promote gluttonous behaviors.

The Biblical Call to Self-Discipline and Holiness

The Bible's teachings on gluttony emphasize the importance of self-discipline and the recognition of the body as a temple of the Holy Spirit. In 1 Corinthians 6:19-20, Paul writes, "What? know ye not that your body is the temple of the Holy Spirit which is in you, which ye have of God, and ye are not your own? For ye are bought with a price: therefore glorify God in your body, and in your spirit, which are God's." This passage underscores the need to honor God by maintaining a healthy and disciplined lifestyle. Gluttony undermines this principle by prioritizing personal pleasure over spiritual and physical well-being. Embracing moderation, making healthier food choices, and seeking to overcome addictive behaviors are practical ways to align with Biblical teachings and promote overall health.

Chapter 8: Idolatry and Greed

"Wherefore, my dearly beloved, flee from idolatry." 1 Corinthians 10:14

Idolatry and greed are deeply interwoven concepts in the Bible, each representing a significant departure from the worship and devotion that God commands. Idolatry, defined as placing material possessions, success, false gods, or even people above God, is explicitly condemned in Scripture. Exodus 20:3-4 provides clear guidance on this issue: "Thou shalt have no other gods before me. Thou shalt not make unto thee any graven image, or any likeness of any thing that is in heaven above, or that is in the earth beneath, or that is in the water under the earth." This commandment underscores the absolute requirement for God to be the sole focus of worship and devotion, prohibiting the elevation of anything or anyone else to His place. Idolatry reflects a misplaced priority, where the created is venerated over the Creator, leading to a distortion of spiritual truth and a breach in the relationship between humanity and God.

False Gods

Worshipping Buddha dolls, Egyptian statues, and Hindu carvings among other things is considered idol worship from a Biblical perspective, as it involves venerating physical representations of deities or spiritual entities rather than the one true God. Exodus 20:4 explicitly forbids the making and worshipping of any "graven image" or likeness of anything in heaven, on earth, or under the sea. These physical objects, whether they are statues or carvings, are intended to represent divine beings or spiritual forces and thus become focal points of worship or reverence. Engaging in such practices is seen as a violation of the commandment to worship only God, reflecting a displacement of divine authority with created images. This form of idolatry is condemned in Scripture as it diverts worship from the Creator to created objects, undermining the fundamental principle of exclusive devotion to God and misaligning one's spiritual focus.

The Spiritual and Moral Implications of Idolatry

The implications of idolatry extend beyond mere worship practices; they penetrate deeply into the spiritual and moral fabric of life. In worshiping false gods or placing undue value on material possessions, individuals are effectively rejecting the sovereignty and supremacy of God. The Bible frequently portrays idolatry as a form of spiritual infidelity. For instance, in Ezekiel 14:3, God accuses His people of setting up idols in their hearts, stating, "Son of man, these men have set up their idols in their heart, and put the stumblingblock of their iniquity before their face." Idolatry involves not only the physical act of idol worship but also a deeper, internal devotion to things that divert one's focus from God. This spiritual betrayal leads to moral decay, as individuals begin to prioritize personal gain or societal status over divine commands, resulting in a life that is misaligned with God's will and purpose.

The Relationship Between Idolatry and Greed

Greed, the excessive pursuit of wealth and possessions at the expense of spiritual well-being, is closely related to idolatry. The Apostle Paul warns against this destructive tendency in 1 Timothy 6:10: "For the love of money is the root of all evil: which while some coveted after, they have erred from the faith, and pierced themselves through with many sorrows." Greed often leads individuals to place their trust and hope in material wealth rather than in God, mirroring the core issue of idolatry. When people allow their desire for financial gain and possessions to overshadow their spiritual life, they effectively make money and material success their ultimate priority, displacing God from His rightful place as the center of their lives. This pursuit not only causes spiritual harm but also leads to a host of practical and ethical issues, including exploitation, corruption, and a diminished sense of community and compassion.

The Path to Overcoming Idolatry and Greed
Overcoming idolatry and greed requires a fundamental shift in priorities and values, grounded in a renewed relationship with God. The Bible calls for a reorientation of the heart and mind towards divine principles and a rejection of materialism. In Matthew 6:24, Jesus teaches, "No man can serve two

masters: for either he will hate the one, and love the other; or else he will hold to the one, and despise the other. Ye cannot serve God and mammon." This passage highlights the impossibility of serving both God and wealth, emphasizing the need to choose one's allegiance. Cultivating a heart of contentment and generosity, as well as focusing on eternal values rather than temporal gains, aligns with Biblical teachings and helps in overcoming the temptations of idolatry and greed. By prioritizing God's kingdom and righteousness, individuals can align their lives with divine purposes and foster a spiritual richness that transcends material possessions.

Righteous Gains

Striving for wealth is not inherently wrong, but the Bible emphasizes that such pursuits must be secondary to seeking the kingdom of God and must be conducted through righteous means. Matthew 6:33 instructs, "But seek ye first the kingdom of God, and his righteousness; and all these things shall be added unto you." This passage underscores the priority of placing God and His righteousness above material wealth. The pursuit of financial success should not overshadow one's commitment to spiritual values and ethical behavior. Wealth gained through dishonest or unethical means is condemned, as seen in Proverbs 10:2, which states, "Treasures of wickedness profit nothing: but righteousness delivereth from death." Therefore, while earning wealth is acceptable, it must be done with integrity and in alignment with Biblical principles, ensuring that financial goals do not compromise one's spiritual priorities or moral conduct.

Chapter 9: Pride and Envy

"For where envying and strife is, there is confusion and every evil work." James 3:16

Pride and envy are two destructive emotions that have profound implications for personal character and relationships. The Bible provides clear warnings about the dangers of these attitudes, highlighting their capacity to disrupt spiritual growth and harm interpersonal dynamics. Proverbs 16:18 states, "Pride goeth before destruction, and an haughty spirit before a fall," illustrating the perilous consequences of arrogance and self-importance. Similarly, James 3:16 notes, "For where envying and strife is, there is confusion and every evil work," emphasizing how envy can lead to chaos and moral decay. Together, these scriptures reveal how pride and envy undermine spiritual well-being and relational harmony, calling for a humility that honors God and fosters genuine respect and love for others.

The Nature and Consequences of Pride

Pride, characterized by an inflated sense of self-importance or arrogance, is a fundamental issue addressed throughout the Bible. Proverbs 16:18 highlights the inherent danger of pride, indicating that it often leads to one's downfall. Pride distorts one's perception of self and others, fostering a sense of superiority that can isolate individuals from meaningful relationships and from God. This self-centered attitude can manifest in various ways, such as boasting, contempt for others, and an unwillingness to acknowledge one's faults. The Bible frequently warns against pride, as it is seen as the root of many sins and a barrier to spiritual growth. For instance, in 1 Peter 5:5, believers are urged to be "clothed with humility: for God resisteth the proud, and giveth grace to the humble." This passage underscores that humility is a virtue that aligns with God's expectations and that pride hinders one's relationship with Him.

The Dangers of Envy

Envy, defined as resentment towards others for their possessions, status, or blessings, also has significant negative consequences. James 3:16 reveals that where envy exists, it brings about confusion and every evil work. Envy distorts one's view of others and their successes, leading to feelings of bitterness and discontent. This resentment can cause interpersonal strife, as envying others can erode trust, foster jealousy, and create divisions. Envy not only affects personal relationships but also impacts one's spiritual life, diverting focus from gratitude and contentment to dissatisfaction and rivalry. The Bible encourages believers to cultivate contentment and rejoice in others' successes, as illustrated in Philippians 4:11, where Paul speaks of learning to be content in all circumstances.

Addressing Pride and Envy Through Biblical Principles

Overcoming pride and envy requires a conscious effort to align one's attitudes with Biblical teachings. Humility is a key antidote to pride, and it involves recognizing one's dependence on God and valuing others above oneself. Jesus exemplified humility throughout His life, and His teachings call believers to follow His example (Philippians 2:3-4). Similarly, combating envy involves cultivating a heart of gratitude and celebrating others' achievements. By focusing on what one has and recognizing the blessings in one's life, individuals can shift their focus away from jealousy and towards a positive and contented outlook. The Bible encourages believers to practice love and kindness, which can counteract the negative effects of pride and envy (1 Corinthians 13:4-5), promoting harmonious relationships and spiritual well-being.

Different Types of Pride

Self-esteem pride and exaggerated self-worth pride, though related to self-perception, represent fundamentally different attitudes towards oneself. Self-esteem refers to a balanced and realistic appreciation of one's abilities and value. It involves recognizing one's strengths and weaknesses with a healthy perspective and understanding that one's worth is intrinsic and not dependent on external validation. This form of self-regard allows individuals to have confidence in their abilities while remaining humble and accepting of their limitations. Healthy self-esteem fosters personal growth, resilience, and positive relationships by encouraging individuals to see themselves as worthy without needing to elevate themselves above others.

In contrast, exaggerated self-worth pride involves an inflated sense of self-importance and superiority over others. This form of pride is characterized by an excessive focus on one's achievements, abilities, or qualities, often at the expense of acknowledging the contributions and value of others. Individuals with exaggerated self-worth pride may engage in boastful behavior, display arrogance, and show a lack of empathy or humility. This attitude can lead to relational conflicts and hinder personal growth, as it prioritizes self-affirmation and validation over genuine self-awareness and respect for others. Unlike self-esteem, which is grounded in reality, exaggerated pride distorts self-perception and can create barriers to meaningful connections and spiritual maturity.

Chapter 10: Anger, Resentment, and Unforgiveness

"Cease from anger, and forsake wrath: fret not thyself in any wise to do evil."
Psalms 37:8

Anger, resentment, and unforgiveness are interconnected emotional states that can profoundly impact both personal well-being and relational dynamics. These feelings often arise from perceived injustices or wrongs and can lead to a cycle of bitterness and conflict. The Bible provides clear guidance on these issues, particularly highlighting the importance of forgiveness. Matthew 6:14-15 states, "For if ye forgive men their trespasses, your heavenly Father will also forgive you: But if ye forgive not men their trespasses, neither will your Father forgive your trespasses." This passage underscores the essential link between forgiving others and receiving forgiveness from God.

Understanding and addressing these emotional states through Biblical teachings is crucial for maintaining spiritual health and fostering harmonious relationships.

The Nature and Impact of Anger and Resentment

Anger and resentment are natural human emotions, but when they are not managed properly, they can become detrimental. Anger, while sometimes justified, can lead to harmful behaviors and attitudes if not addressed constructively. Proverbs 29:11 advises, "A fool uttereth all his mind: but a wise man keepeth it in till afterwards." This verse suggests that uncontrolled anger can lead to foolish actions and words, while wise individuals exercise restraint and manage their emotions. Resentment, a lingering feeling of displeasure or indignation, often arises when individuals perceive that they have been wronged and are unable to resolve their grievances. Both anger and resentment can lead to a hardened heart and an unwillingness to forgive, creating barriers to reconciliation and personal peace.

The Consequences of Unforgiveness

Unforgiveness, characterized by holding grudges and refusing to let go of past hurts, has serious spiritual and relational consequences. Matthew 6:14-15 highlights that forgiveness is not optional for believers; it is a fundamental aspect of receiving God's forgiveness. When individuals choose not to forgive, they obstruct their own spiritual growth and relational harmony. Unforgiveness can perpetuate a cycle of bitterness, conflict, and division, leading to strained relationships and emotional distress. Ephesians 4:31-32 provides practical advice on dealing with these issues: "Let all bitterness, and wrath, and anger, and clamor, and evil speaking, be put away from you, with all malice: And be ye kind one to another, tenderhearted, forgiving one another, even as God for Christ's sake hath forgiven you." This passage emphasizes that releasing bitterness and practicing forgiveness is crucial for maintaining healthy relationships and reflecting God's grace.

The Path to Forgiveness and Healing

Addressing anger, resentment, and unforgiveness requires a deliberate and often challenging process of personal and spiritual transformation. Forgiveness begins with acknowledging the hurt and choosing to release the hold that anger and resentment have on one's heart. This process is supported by seeking God's help through prayer, studying Scripture, and practicing empathy. Colossians 3:13 instructs, "Forbearing one another, and forgiving one another, if any man have a quarrel against any: even as Christ forgave you, so also do ye." This verse highlights the importance of mirroring Christ's forgiveness in our interactions with others. By adopting a posture of humility and grace, individuals can move beyond their grievances and experience healing and reconciliation. Forgiveness is not merely a one-time act but an ongoing commitment to maintaining a heart of grace and mercy, aligned with Biblical teachings.

Chapter 11: Gossip, Slander, and Foul Language

"Keep thy tongue from evil, and thy lips from speaking guile." Psalms 34:13

Gossip, slander, and foul language are pervasive issues that have existed for centuries, but in today's digital age, they have taken on new forms and have become even more widespread due to the ease and speed of communication facilitated by social media. Speaking ill of others, spreading rumors, damaging reputations, and using offensive language can have severe consequences for individuals and communities alike. The Bible provides clear guidance on this issue, as stated in Ephesians 4:29 "Let no corrupt communication proceed out of your mouth, but that which is good to the use of edifying." This verse underscores the importance of using words to build up rather than tear down, highlighting the moral imperative to avoid gossip, slander, and foul language.

The Nature and Impact of Gossip, Slander, and Foul Language

Gossip involves sharing information about someone, often without their knowledge or consent, which can harm their reputation and relationships. Slander, a more malicious form of gossip, entails making false statements with the intent to damage someone's character. Both behaviors stem from a desire to elevate oneself at the expense of others, driven by envy, insecurity, or a simple lack of consideration for the impact of one's words.

Foul language, characterized by the use of offensive or vulgar words, further exacerbates the damage caused by gossip and slander. It can demean, belittle, and humiliate individuals, stripping them of their dignity. The consequences of these actions can be devastating, leading to broken relationships, loss of trust, and emotional distress for the individuals targeted. Proverbs 16:28 states, "A froward man soweth strife: and a whisperer separateth chief friends," emphasizing the divisive nature of such actions.

The Role of Social Media

In the contemporary world, social media platforms have magnified the reach and impact of gossip, slander, and foul language. With the click of a button, rumors, false statements, and offensive language can spread to thousands or even millions of people, often with little regard for their veracity or the harm they may cause. The anonymity and impersonal nature of online interactions can embolden individuals to say things they might not otherwise express in face-to-face conversations. The rapid dissemination of information on social media makes it challenging to retract or correct false statements and offensive remarks once they are released into the public domain. This environment can create a breeding ground for harmful communication, making it all the more essential for individuals to exercise restraint and responsibility in their online interactions.

Biblical Guidance and the Call to Edify

The Bible offers clear guidance on how believers should use their words. Ephesians 4:29 admonishes disciples to refrain from corrupt communication, including gossip, slander, and foul language, and instead speak in ways that edify others. This means using language that builds up, encourages, and supports rather than tearing down and causing harm. James 3:5-6 further illustrates the power of the tongue, comparing it to a small fire that can set a great forest ablaze, highlighting the profound impact words can have. Practicing self-control and choosing to speak kindly and truthfully are vital aspects of living a life that honors God and respects others.

Overcoming the Temptation of Gossip, Slander, and Foul Language

Addressing the issue of gossip, slander, and foul language requires a conscious effort to align one's behavior with Biblical principles. This involves cultivating a heart of empathy and compassion, understanding the potential harm that careless and offensive words can cause. It also requires accountability, both personally and within a community, encouraging others to speak positively and refrain from spreading harmful information and using foul language. Prayer and reflection can help individuals seek God's guidance in using their words wisely, fostering a spirit of love and respect. By making a deliberate choice to use words that edify, individuals can contribute to a more positive and supportive community, both online and offline.

Chapter 12: Cheating and Stealing

"Let him that stole steal no more: but rather let him labour, working with his hands the thing which is good, that he may have to give to him that needeth." Ephesians 4:28

Cheating and stealing are sins that are universally condemned across cultures. These acts undermine trust, disrupt social harmony, and erode personal integrity. The Bible clearly instructs against such behaviors, as seen in Exodus 20:15 "Thou shalt not steal." Despite this clear moral directive, people often rationalize their dishonest actions, particularly in contexts like petty theft from a job or company, believing them to be inconsequential. However, these rationalizations fail to acknowledge the broader implications of such behavior on individual character and societal trust.

The Nature and Impact of Cheating and Stealing

Cheating involves acts of dishonesty or deceit to gain an unfair advantage, whether in academics, business, relationships, or other areas of life. Stealing, on the other hand, is the act of taking something that does not belong to oneself, depriving the rightful owner of their property or resources. Both actions are fundamentally rooted in selfishness and a disregard for the rights and well-being of others. The immediate impacts of these actions can include financial loss, emotional distress, and damaged relationships.

In the workplace, for instance, stealing office supplies or falsifying hours worked might seem minor, but it creates an atmosphere of mistrust and sets a precedent for further dishonest behavior. Over time, such actions can lead to a culture of corruption and dishonesty, where integrity is sacrificed for personal gain.

Rationalizing Petty Theft

People often rationalize petty theft by downplaying its significance or justifying it as a response to perceived injustices, such as feeling underpaid or undervalued at work. However, these rationalizations overlook the fundamental ethical breach involved. Stealing, regardless of scale, is a violation of trust and a breach of moral principles. Proverbs 10:2 states, "Treasures of wickedness profit nothing: but righteousness delivereth from death," emphasizing that ill-gotten gains ultimately bring no true benefit. When individuals justify minor acts of theft, they undermine their own integrity and contribute to a broader culture of dishonesty. This rationalization can lead to more significant ethical compromises over time, as the boundary between right and wrong becomes increasingly blurred.

The Erosion of Trust

Trust is the foundation of all healthy relationships and functioning communities. When individuals cheat or steal, they break this trust, causing harm that extends beyond the immediate victim. In professional settings, for instance, a single act of theft can lead to increased scrutiny and suspicion among colleagues, reducing overall morale and productivity. Employers may implement stricter policies and surveillance, creating an environment of mistrust and tension.

On a larger scale, widespread dishonesty and theft can erode public trust in institutions and societal systems, leading to cynicism and disengagement. The Bible calls for honesty and integrity, as seen in Ephesians 4:28 "Let him that stole steal no more: but rather let him labour, working with his hands the thing which is good, that he may have to give to him that needeth."

Restoring Integrity and Trust

Overcoming the temptation to cheat or steal requires a commitment to ethical principles and a willingness to address underlying motivations. This begins with recognizing the inherent value of honesty and the long-term benefits of maintaining integrity. Building a culture of trust involves creating environments where ethical behavior is rewarded and supported, and where individuals feel valued and fairly treated. On a personal level, individuals can seek guidance from spiritual teachings, such as those found in the Bible, to reinforce the importance of honesty. Regular self-reflection and accountability can help individuals stay true to their values, even in challenging situations. Repentance and making amends for past wrongs are also crucial steps in restoring trust and integrity.

Maintaining a Good Reputation

A good name, esteemed for its association with integrity, honesty, and trustworthiness, is valued more than material wealth and possessions. Proverbs 22:1 emphasizes this principle, stating, "A good name is rather to be chosen than great riches, and loving favour rather than silver and gold." A reputation built on ethical conduct and moral character garners respect and trust, fostering meaningful relationships and opening doors to opportunities that money cannot buy. The enduring legacy of a good name outlasts fleeting material gains, underscoring its paramount importance in the pursuit of a virtuous and impactful life.

Chapter 13: Neglecting Responsibilities

"Now he that planteth and he that watereth
are one: and every man shall receive his
own reward according to his own labour."
1 Corinthians 3:8

Neglecting responsibilities is a serious issue that affects both our personal lives and our relationship with God. This neglect often stems from laziness, lack of motivation, or a failure to understand the importance of our duties. Falling short of what God wants us to do, especially in critical areas such as parenting, is not only a personal failing but a sin that has profound consequences. The Bible emphasizes the importance of diligence and faithfulness in fulfilling our responsibilities, as highlighted in Colossians 3:23 "And whatsoever ye do, do it heartily, as to the Lord, and not unto men."

Doing God's will is a fundamental aspect of living a believer. It involves aligning our actions and decisions with God's commands and purposes, which are often revealed through Scripture, prayer, and our conscience. Our conscience, guided by the Holy Spirit, serves as an internal compass, helping us discern right from wrong and prompting us toward righteous actions. Romans 12:2 emphasizes the transformation needed to discern God's will: "And be not conformed to this world: but be ye transformed by the renewing of your mind, that ye may prove what is that good, and acceptable, and perfect, will of God." By listening to our conscience, we can stay attuned to God's direction and make choices that reflect His love and righteousness.

Utilizing our God-given gifts to serve Him and humanity is another crucial aspect of fulfilling God's will. Each individual is endowed with unique talents and abilities intended for the greater good and the advancement of God's kingdom. 1 Peter 4:10 states, "As every man hath received the gift, even so minister the same one to another, as good stewards of the manifold grace of God." This verse underscores the responsibility to use our gifts to serve others, demonstrating God's grace through our actions. Whether through acts of kindness, teaching, leadership, or other forms of service, employing our talents in God's service enriches our lives and the lives of those around us. By doing so, we fulfill our divine purpose and contribute to the manifestation of God's love and will on earth.

The Importance of Responsibility

Responsibility is a fundamental aspect of a faithful life serving God. It involves fulfilling the duties and obligations entrusted to us by

God, whether in our personal lives, our families, or our communities. These responsibilities are opportunities to serve God and others, reflecting His love and character in our actions. Neglecting these duties not only impacts our relationship with God but also affects those around us. Jesus taught the importance of being faithful in our responsibilities in the Parable of the Talents (Matthew 25:14-30), where the faithful servants are rewarded for their diligence, while the lazy servant faces condemnation for his neglect.

Neglecting Parental Responsibilities

Laziness and lack of motivation can lead to significant neglect of responsibilities, with particularly severe consequences in the context of parenting. Parents have a God-given duty to care for, nurture, and guide their children, raising them in the knowledge and fear of the Lord. Neglecting this responsibility can lead to physical, emotional, and spiritual harm for the children. Proverbs 22:6 states, "Train up a child in the way he should go: and when he is old, he will not depart from it." Failing to provide proper care, guidance, and love can result in children feeling abandoned, unloved, and unguided, potentially leading them to stray from the path of righteousness.

Parents are entrusted to protect their child from the womb. The sin of abortion is a grievous violation of the sanctity of human life, which is a gift from God. Scripture affirms the value and dignity of life from conception, as illustrated in Psalm 139:13-16 "For thou hast possessed my reins: thou hast covered me in my mother's womb. I will praise thee; for I am fearfully and wonderfully made." Taking the life of an unborn child is seen as an act that contradicts God's commandment, "Thou shalt not kill" (Exodus 20:13). Abortion not only ends an innocent life but also inflicts deep spiritual and emotional wounds on those involved. Disciples are called to protect and cherish life at all stages, advocating for alternatives that honor the value of both the unborn and the mother, and seeking forgiveness and healing for those affected by this sin.

Neglecting financial responsibility with children is a serious failing that directly impacts their well-being and development. Providing for children's needs, including food, clothing, education, and shelter, is a fundamental parental duty. The Bible underscores this responsibility in 1 Timothy 5:8 "But if any provide not for his own, and specially for those of his own house, he hath denied the faith, and is worse than an infidel." Failing to fulfill this obligation can lead to significant hardships for children, hindering their growth and potential. It also sets a poor example of stewardship and responsibility, potentially influencing the children's own values and behaviors. Ultimately, neglecting financial responsibility toward one's children not only harms them but also represents a profound neglect of one's God-given duties as a parent.

Neglecting parental responsibilities is not just a personal failing; it is a sin against God's commands. Ephesians 6:4 instructs, "And, ye fathers, provoke not your children to wrath: but bring them up in the nurture and admonition of the Lord." This verse underscores the importance of active and loving involvement in a child's upbringing. When parents fail to fulfill this role, they are not only neglecting their children but also disobeying God's directives, which can have eternal consequences for both the parents and the children.

Being a Burden to Society

Not working and being dependent on a system or others, when one is capable of labor, is considered a sin according to Biblical principles. The Bible emphasizes the importance of diligence and hard work, as reflected in 2 Thessalonians 3:10 "For even when we were with you, this we commanded you, that if any would not work, neither should he eat." This verse highlights the expectation that individuals should contribute to their own sustenance and not rely on others when they are able to work. Laziness and unwillingness to work can lead to a life of idleness, which is condemned in scripture, as it not only burdens others but also neglects the God-given duty to be productive and responsible.

Living in dependence on others or a system, when one is fully capable of working, goes against the Biblical mandate of stewardship and self-sufficiency. Proverbs 6:6-11 uses the example of the ant to teach the value of hard work and preparation: "Go to the ant, thou sluggard; consider her ways, and be wise: Which having no guide, overseer, or ruler, provideth her meat in the summer, and gathereth her food in the harvest." This passage illustrates that even the smallest creatures demonstrate industriousness and foresight, setting an example for humans to follow. By choosing not to work and relying on others, individuals fail to fulfill their responsibilities and contribute to society, ultimately dishonoring God's design for a diligent and purposeful life.

Overcoming Neglect and Embracing Responsibility

Addressing the sin of neglecting responsibilities requires a sincere commitment to change and a reliance on God's strength and guidance. It begins with repentance, acknowledging the areas where one has fallen short and seeking God's forgiveness. Prayer and scripture study are essential in renewing one's mind and aligning one's priorities with God's will. Philippians 4:13 reminds us, "I can do all things through Christ which strengtheneth me." Through Christ, believers can find the strength and motivation to overcome laziness and fulfill their responsibilities diligently.

In practical terms, parents and individuals must establish routines and habits that prioritize their responsibilities. This includes setting aside time for family, actively engaging in children's lives, and seeking to model Christ-like behavior. Accountability partners, whether friends, family, or members of a faith community, can provide encouragement and support in this journey. It is also important to seek God's guidance through prayer, asking for wisdom and strength to fulfill one's duties faithfully.

Chapter 14: Trashy Entertainment

"And have no fellowship with the unfruitful works of darkness, but rather reprove them." Ephesians 5:11

In today's culture, many forms of entertainment, such as certain music, movies, and activities, promote values that are contrary to Biblical principles. These trashy forms of entertainment often glorify immorality, violence, and perversion, subtly influencing our thoughts and actions. As Disciples in Christ, it is crucial to recognize the detrimental impact of such entertainment and to seek repentance, aligning our lives with the purity and holiness that God desires.

The Detrimental Impact of Trashy Entertainment

Trashy entertainment can desensitize individuals to sin, making behaviors that were once considered shocking or immoral seem acceptable. Music with explicit lyrics, movies with graphic content, and activities that celebrate vice can gradually erode our moral compass. Philippians 4:8 advises, "Finally, brethren, whatsoever things are true, whatsoever things are honest, whatsoever things are just, whatsoever things are pure, whatsoever things are lovely, whatsoever things are of good report; if there be any virtue, and if there be any praise, think on these things." Consuming entertainment that is contrary to these virtues can lead us away from God's truth and distort our perception of right and wrong.

Moreover, such forms of entertainment often promote a lifestyle that is in stark contrast to the teachings of Christ. They can glorify promiscuity, materialism, and a hedonistic approach to life, which can become stumbling blocks in our spiritual journey. By immersing ourselves in these influences, we risk adopting attitudes and behaviors that are incompatible with a Christ-centered life. Romans 12:2 instructs us to transform our minds and live according to God's will. We must critically evaluate and often reject entertainment that contradicts His teachings.

The Call to Repentance

Repentance is a fundamental aspect of a Christ centered life, involving a sincere turning away from sin and towards God. Recognizing the negative influence of trashy entertainment is the first step towards repentance. It requires a conscious decision to reject these forms of media and activities, seeking instead that which edifies and aligns with God's standards. 1 John 1:9 assures us, "If we confess our sins, he is faithful and just to forgive us our sins, and to cleanse us from all unrighteousness." By confessing our participation in harmful entertainment and committing to change, we open ourselves to God's cleansing and transformative power.

In addition to personal repentance, it is important to encourage others, especially within our families and communities, to discern the impact of their entertainment choices. Teaching children and young people about the importance of consuming media that upholds Christ's values can help them develop a strong moral foundation. Ephesians 5:11 advises, "And have no fellowship with the unfruitful works of darkness, but rather reprove them." By collectively rejecting trashy entertainment and promoting wholesome alternatives, we create an environment that nurtures spiritual growth and honors God.

Embracing Wholesome Alternatives

Repentance from trashy forms of entertainment is not merely about rejection but also about embracing that which uplifts and edifies. There are numerous forms of music, movies, and activities that inspire, teach, and reinforce positive values. Faith-based music and films as well as activities that promote community and service can fill the void left by rejecting harmful entertainment. These alternatives not only entertain but also strengthen our faith and bring us closer to God.

Engaging in wholesome entertainment can also serve as a witness to others. When we choose media that reflects our faith, we demonstrate the joy and fulfillment that comes from living according to God's principles. Matthew 5:16 encourages us, "Let your light so shine before men, that they may see your good works, and glorify your Father which is in heaven." By making choices that honor God, we can influence those around us and draw them towards a more righteous and fulfilling way of life.

Chapter 15: Conclusion

Repentance is the cornerstone of a life aligned with God's will, a crucial practice that ensures our spiritual health and prepares us for eternity. While this book has addressed various sins—ranging from dishonesty and idolatry to sexual immorality and neglecting responsibilities—it is essential to recognize that our examination is not exhaustive. Each individual must engage in sincere self-reflection, seeking the guidance of the Holy Spirit to identify and renounce their unique failings. It is through this process of repentance that we draw nearer to God, experience His transformative power, and embrace the fullness of His grace and mercy.

Human nature is adept at deception, capable of fooling others and even ourselves about the true state of our hearts. However, God, who sees all and knows all, is the ultimate judge of our lives. Hebrews 4:13 reminds us, "Neither is there any creature that is not manifest in his sight: but all things are naked and opened unto the eyes of him with whom we have to do." Our actions and intentions are laid bare before Him, and it is His judgment that determines our eternal destiny. It is a sobering reality that compels us to live with integrity, humility, and an ever-present awareness of our need for His forgiveness.

The call to repentance is urgent and non-negotiable, as the Kingdom of God is at hand. Jesus Himself proclaimed this message at the outset of His ministry, emphasizing its critical importance. Matthew 4:17 states, "From that time Jesus began to preach, and to say, Repent: for the kingdom of heaven is at hand." This divine mandate urges us to be wise, to fear God, and to turn away from sin. Repentance is not merely an act of contrition but a profound reorientation of our lives toward God's will. It involves a heartfelt sorrow for our sins, a determination to change, and a commitment to live in obedience to God's commandments.

In conclusion, the practice of repentance is indispensable for every believer. It is the pathway to forgiveness, restoration, and eternal life. As we reflect on our lives, let us be diligent in seeking God's guidance, confessing our sins, and making the necessary changes to align ourselves with His will. By doing so, we honor God, enrich our spiritual lives, and secure our place in His eternal Kingdom. Let us heed the call to repentance with urgency and sincerity, recognizing that our ultimate fate lies in the hands of a just and merciful God. Be wise, fear God, and repent, for the Kingdom of God is indeed at hand.

About the Author

Karajah Yashar, an accomplished author and academic, holds a degree from Rutgers University and has an impressive professional background. His career includes roles at prestigious institutions such as Rutgers University and the University of Central Florida. In addition to his academic positions, he has also made significant contributions through teaching and counseling with organizations like The Transition House and the Orange County Public School system. His diverse experiences have equipped him with a rich understanding of both educational and spiritual matters, which he has leveraged to positively impact numerous lives.

In 2016, Karajah Yashar founded Blackstone Publishing, an Orlando-based publishing house dedicated to disseminating scholarly Biblical works. This venture underscores his commitment to spreading theological knowledge and fostering a deeper understanding of the Bible. Karajah's life took a transformative turn in 2001 when he experienced his rebirth in Christ. Since then, he has dedicated himself to doing Christ's work and making disciples, a mission that permeates his professional and personal endeavors.

www.ingramcontent.com/pod-product-compliance
Lightning Source LLC
Chambersburg PA
CBHW071009120626
46546CB00003B/1009